SURVIVAL

SURVIVAL

KOLLIN L. TAYLOR

authorHOUSE®

AuthorHouse™ LLC
1663 Liberty Drive
Bloomington, IN 47403
www.authorhouse.com
Phone: 1-800-839-8640

Published by AuthorHouse 01/09/2014

ISBN: 978-1-4918-5005-3 (sc)
ISBN: 978-1-4918-5011-4 (e)

Library of Congress Control Number: 2014900571

Dedication

This book is dedicated to survivors of sexual assault and to everyone who helped them during their recovery. A very special thank you to survivors who reach out to others in an effort to prevent sexual assault, to assist survivors in their recovery, and to bring the guilty to justice.

Table of Contents

Acknowledgments

God, I wish there was no such thing as sexual assault. I have long questioned why it happens. I still don't know, but I am amazed that a number of survivors do not blame You for their being assaulted. Instead, they thank You for saving them. They also thank You for giving them the courage to come forward and, in some cases, confront their attackers. Most perpetrators are not incarcerated, due in part to the fact that some people do not report that they have been sexually assaulted, but You ensure that the perpetrators do not go unpunished in the long run.

Docuramafilms and Cinedigm Entertainment Group, thanks for making *The Invisible War* (http://www.invisiblewarmovie.com/). Some view it as an indictment against the military, but I view it as enlightening. The film shows that what happens in civilian society also happens in the military.

Investigation Discovery, thanks for airing *Surviving Evil* (http://investigation.discovery.com/tv-shows/surviving-evil). It is a source of inspiration and a testimony to our strength to survive life's challenges.

Tasha Pernell and Christine Hale, thanks for everything you do to assist members of the military community.

Sterlin King, thank you very much for your generosity, for which I'm eternally grateful.

Special thanks to every survivor who shared his or her story of survival with me over the years. I did not share your story in this book because I won't betray your trust. I am honored that you trusted me and revealed the things you did. I hope that our conversation gave you the courage to share your story with the person with whom you choose to spend your life.

Introduction

I have long held the belief that one of the most despicable things a person can do is commit sexual assault against another person. A sexual assault is not an easy thing to recover from. Unfortunately, survivors often live with a greater sense of guilt and shame than perpetrators do. This is partly because survivors suffer in silence. It was while watching the documentary *The Invisible War,* wherein survivors spoke out against sexual assaults and the criminals who committed them, that I was inspired to give a voice to those who are sometimes afraid to speak up. The film inspired me to write six poems. I thought I was simply going to add them to another of my poetry books. However, God had started something, and He completes whatever He starts. It sometimes takes me as little as two days to finish writing a book of poetry. But *Survival* took me two months to write, and I don't consider it to be complete. There are more stories to tell. Individuals who have been the victims of this heinous crime in many ways embody what it means to be a survivor. Some of the other poems in this collection were inspired by Investigation Discovery's *Surviving Evil,* which is hosted by Charisma Carpenter, a survivor of an attempted rape. Attempted rape can be just as traumatic as rape itself. In this collection, I also touch on the stories of people from all over the world.

Survival is a collection of poetry that takes you on a journey. You will see just how much some people have had to overcome, and you will discover that, even though it is not always easy, life does and will continue to go on.

Stuck in Time

I was the sacrificial lamb
Who was preyed upon by an alpha ram.
My boss thought that I was creating drama,
But I was really suffering from sexual trauma.

Now my recovery is predicated
On my being heavily medicated.
Years later, it cuts deeper than a knife
When I relive the most frightening time of my life.

The perpetrator walks around with a feeling of invincibility
While my pain is shrouded in invisibility.

Note: Inspired by the film *The Invisible War*.

Repeat Offender

I wish I would've run on the double.
On day one, I knew I was in trouble.
My intuition had me reeling
And had left me with an ominous feeling.

A few days later, I wished I was dead.
I was defiled. He had put a pillow over my head.
Long afterward, I remained shocked and sore.
Would you believe that he came back for more?

I know his scent better than I know his name.
He filled me with shame.
I reported to others this hurtful information,
But it only led to my character's defamation.

Note: Inspired by the film *The Invisible War.*

Piece of Meat

On day one, they turned up the heat.
Once a person, I am now a piece of meat.
They dehumanized me, really slapped it on thick,
By warning me about wearing skirts and lipstick.

Day one: it already feels like I'm doing hard time.
Being a woman is my only crime.
I tried to reason by saying, "Look, mister!
What if this was how someone treated your mother, wife, daughter, or sister?"

Note: Inspired by the film *The Invisible War.*

"It Won't Happen to Me!"

Most men say, "It won't happen to me!"
But then they're stripped of their dignity.
One of my friends had hardened his body parts
From years of practicing martial arts.

Now, his life is not the same.
He still wrestles with the pain.
Every day, he wishes he was dead
Because of what happened after he was hit over the head.

They held him down and stripped him of his humility
Once they had removed his cloak of invincibility.

Note: Inspired by the film *The Invisible War.*

Ice-Cold

In the middle of the night I heard the yell.
My baby was reliving her hell.
Everyone in the house awoke when she screamed.
She was having painful memories, not having a dream.

I accepted her in marriage, to have and to hold,
But now she freezes up. When I approach her, she is cold.
She's a delicate flower that I must handle with care,
But my love for her doesn't eradicate her fear.

Will she ever get better? Will this ever end?
I would die celibate rather than abandon my wife and friend.

Note: Inspired by the film *The Invisible War.*

Worst Crime

Ever since the beginning of time,
Sexual assault has been the worst crime.
I would prefer death
Over remembering the odor of your breath.

In some places, rape is weapon of war.
It leaves a permanent scar.
Even if it's a scar that others can't see,
It's a reminder of the despicable things you did to me.

But, for as long as I live,
I'll have things that no one can take away. They're mine to give.

Note: Inspired by the film *The Invisible War.*

The Will to Live

Growing up, she must have felt hated.
It seemed that her future had been decimated.
She wanted to belong to another,
As she hadn't felt loved by her mother.

Then—consider it a curse—
Her grandmother's boyfriend made her life worse.
She wasn't able to escape him or find a place to hide.
While he defiled her, she hid herself deep inside.

She worked a double shift one day
And was happy that she had a job and could keep out of his way.
It also gave her time to write
A good-bye note before committing suicide that night.
She had nothing left for which she wanted to live;
He had taken what was hers alone to give.

As she rode her bicycle home in the dark,
Her life was changed after a stranger placed his car in park.
It was as if her heart had been pierced by a gunshot
When he kidnapped her in the church parking lot.

He drove around with her behind a blindfold,
But everything she sensed was hers to hold.
She made note of things she could hear, feel, and smell,
And of the little she could glimpse as well.

He took her out of the car, but she dared not run,
Because she remembered the cold steel of his gun.
A minute must have felt like an hour
When he took her home and washed her in the shower.
His seeing her naked body made her ill and intimated.
Though he hadn't touched her yet, she was already violated.

Then he treated her with disdain
As he repeatedly defiled her and inflicted searing pain.
But there was something that he never knew.
What he was doing was something she had already been through.
Even though he shook her rattle,
The Lord had prepared her for this battle.

He gave her all that her body could take,
Inflicting psychological trauma with nary a break.
But one of the things that she most feared
Was turning up missing and no one cared.
She blew an emotional fuse
When they mentioned that she was missing on the news.

He learned from the newscast that she was young in age.
Then her tears filled him with rage.
This young woman who had planned her death
Was determined to fight and prevent this man from taking her last breath.

Then he told her to be quiet as he brandished his gun.

So she opened up that familiar place inside herself and told her emotions to run.

And to add to his plate of disgrace,

He told her to caress his face.

But even though she was blindfolded and couldn't see,

She committed details about him to memory.

If he was going to wipe her off the earth's face,

At least she will have left evidence of her existence all over his place.

He decided that he couldn't go much further.

In the past, this meant that he then committed murder.

She offered herself to him, but he said no.

Instead, he drove her across town and let her go.

She wasn't sure what he planned to do.

Dare she believe that her nightmare was through?

The thing that stays in my memory
Is the fact that she said, "God saved me!"
Despite her life's grief,
She was a young woman with such faith, such belief.

The police were hot on the kidnapper's case,
But the red fiber from his car was their only trace.
After the police failed to catch him in a trap,
God put a key piece of evidence into their lap.

The young woman, first thing after her apparent condemnation,
Ran to the nearest police station.
To add to her grief,
The police regarded her with disbelief.
They couldn't believe that she had experienced something so wrong,
Because she was so calm and seemingly strong.

Their refusal to believe her caused her to shut down and feel
defeated.
Then one officer gained her trust, so she repeated
The details of her story,
Those about the route, the evidence, and the scene, which were
gory.

While the police initially failed,
A few days later a serial murderer and rapist was jailed.
To add to our sense of satisfaction,
Her grandmother's boyfriend was taken out of action.

I end this discourse
With the news that this woman is now a member of the police
force.
Now she puts people like him in jail
And tells survivors that they will prevail.

Note: Inspired by Investigation Discovery's *Surviving Evil.*

Lucky Day

I can't undo history
Or get rid of the memory.
There's still a price to pay
Even though I got away.

I remember how you undressed me with your eyes
And stared between my thighs.
My efforts were for naught
As we furiously fought.

The end result was clear.
My friends weren't near.
It was like a bad dream
Where I couldn't scream.

So, even though on that day you didn't win,
I retain scars from what might've been.

Note: Inspired by Investigation Discovery's *Surviving Evil.*

Whac-a-Mole

I thought that I had forgotten what happened that day.
I thought that I had locked the pain away.
I buried the pain deep inside my soul,
But it was a game of whac-a-mole.

What I thought I had left in the past
Told me, "Not so fast!"
Memories of the event may have been repressed,
But the aftereffects are silently expressed.

Then I finally faced my fears
And released what had eaten away at me for years.
Although my eyes were temporarily wetter,
My life today is so much better.

How Did I Get Here?

How did I get here?!
The last thing I remember was being there.
Let me think . . .
The last thing I remember is my drink.

Despite feeling so heavily medicated,
I still sense, somehow, that I was penetrated.
Do I have bloodshot eyes
Or are those bruises between my thighs?!

I feel like I was punched in the nose.
Where am I? And where are my clothes?!

"Honeymoon"

Our honeymoon was filled with magic,
But then things became tragic.
It evolved into the worst day of my life
Because I had failed my wife.

Haunting memories replay in my head.
They defiled her on our hotel room's bed.
Now we're going home soon
With crimson red draped over our honeymoon.

You're still the one I adore.
Will you respect me anymore?

Failed!

I'm glad that later he was jailed.
But I still failed.
I'm haunted by my dreams.
I can't stop your screams.

I can still hear your plea.
You had said, "Please, help me!"
But it was no use
Because I couldn't get my bloody ankles and wrists loose.

Even though "nothing" happened to me,
I have PTSD.

Healing Hugs

It was me and you against ten
Very savage men.
Their intentions were clear to see,
But I thought they wanted you, not me.

The thing that plagues my memory
Is that they made you watch what they did to me.
I was relieved when they fled, the thugs
Most of all, I loved your healing hugs.

Shame on You

The details are very gory,
But I won't tell the whole story.
I refuse to keep the truth inside
As you walk around, filled with pride.

I'm going to tell the world your name
And cast upon you the requisite shame.
You counted on my silence
After your act of violence.

For some, it's a last resort,
But I'll see you in court.

The Cycle

I feel like such a loser.

I was abused, and now I'm an abuser.

I remember how I felt.

But, now, just look at the pain I myself have dealt.

Really, how could this be?

How could I do the despicable things that were done to me?

Disgusted

The first time I did it, I had gotten away,
Even though I felt sick all day.
Instead of getting better, though, I became the worst.
I had developed an unquenchable thirst.

My victims wanted only for it to end;
They promised to tell no one, not even a friend.
But then for me it became a thrill.
After I violated them, I made a threat to kill.

As time went on, I no longer felt disgusted,
Not even when I was finally busted.
One person's testimony sent me to jail.
In the end, justice will prevail.

Crossed the Line

You and I were in the friend zone,
But I wanted to get into your end zone.
I'm not talking about the sexual part.
What I always wanted to access was your heart.
I knew you were about to go away,
And there was so much left that I wanted to say.
Then you really lit my fire.
I was overcome with sexual desire.
I wanted to light your flame
So you would give me a special name.
I wanted to make my presence felt
By making your heart melt.
We'd always been cool about spending time alone
Because we were comfortable in the friend zone.

But then came the night
When I wanted to love you right.
I wanted to leave your world rocked.
But when you screamed and froze, I was shocked.
I stopped and stepped back across the line,
But that didn't mean that things were fine.
I left after I apologized to you.
I was shocked when the police came by for an interview.

You were the one whom I wished I had dated,
But my attempt to get closer to you only got me incarcerated.

I Know How You Feel

I never cared about the pain they felt.
In fact, I rejoiced when it was dealt.
I wasn't seeking treasure;
Hurting others was my pleasure.

But that was then, and this is now.
The Lord had gotten to me somehow.
Where others had miserably failed,
He was the one who prevailed.

There were certain things I didn't care to know,
But then He gave me a show.
I learned lessons that I'll never forget.
Now I'm filled with regret.

I had left so many feeling disgusted
Before I was busted.
I thought, while being processed, that this marked my worst day,
But now the booking room is where I wished I could stay.
A man will find what he seeks,
But they found nothing when they asked me to spread my cheeks.
My dignity wasn't the only thing the guards took
When they subjected my private parts to a thorough look.
The air suddenly became thicker

When they started to snicker.
Then they gave me an ominous clue
When they said, "May God help you."
Then they simply blew my mind
When they asked, "Do you know how they treat your kind?"

The other prisoners performed an incredible feat

By making me feel like a piece of dead meat.

I'll spare you all the gruesome facts,

But I will tell you that they had me perform some unforgettable acts.

They said they were not gay

Even though they did me that way.

My case got even worse

When one of my victims served as my nurse.

She said, "Do not fear,

I'll still give you the very best care."

Things got even more real

When she said, "You hurt me once so I know how you feel."

Gangs

The situation in India is a mess.
There are so many stories about it in the press.
Women are raped by gangs
Of violent men who have fangs.

It's a disturbing trend
That I pray will come to an end.
It's bad enough for one person to commit that crime,
But it must be hell to go through it time after time.

Some women didn't survive.
Others don't feel lucky to be alive.

Fighting Spirit

Hers was a fighting spirit that was so strong,
Despite everything that he had done wrong.
After he defiled her that night,
He used acid to end her plight.

After he had left her for dead,
She found herself in a hospital bed.
He had tried to take her last breath,
But her fighting spirit wasn't ready for death.

So, as a reward for everything he did that was wrong,
He ended up imprisoned with a cellmate who was big and strong.

Vulture

This man was worse than a vulture.
He would be regarded as a bottom-feeder by the people of any culture.
How can you come across someone who had been defiled,
And instead of helping, you helped yourself and then smiled?

Something worse than not helping a survivor you found
Is kicking that person further to the ground.
I can't believe you saw someone who was battered and bruised
And thought it good that she be further abused.

She had just started on the road to recovery
Before you inflicted even more misery.

The Sitter

This person has barely been alive.
She was sexually abused before she turned five.
You should have seen your eyes
And their look of surprise
When you were caught in the act.
Vengeance, then, we tried to exact.

Initially, it was an assault and battery case
Until the district attorney entered the space.
It's not that we were justified;
It's what happened when other parents were notified.

A predator was on the loose:
A babysitter whose motive was sexual abuse.

Fe-Male

Before the Falls of Niagara,
I was given roofies and Viagra.
You were a lady I had just met.
I told you I was celibate.

I told you about my faith, and you understood,
But little did I know that you were up to no good.
I was a man who woke up, bounded by duct tape.
Tears came to my eyes; I was a victim of rape.

It doesn't matter if you were someone I would've dated.
Yes, I'm a man, but I was violated.
I wanted to put the horse before the carriage,
So I was saving myself for marriage.

The only thing worse than my feeling of shame
Was the fact that the police didn't treat a male survivor the same.

Have Fun

I thought this was something that only happened in a prison cell.
But, truly, I have a roommate from hell.
I remember the girls you brought home—and that the walls were thin.
What's this pain you're inflicting?

I hope you're back there having fun,
Because, for the rest of your life, you'd better run.
Even though right now I prefer death,
Vengeance will be mine before I take my last breath.

For this, you'll probably end up in hell.
I'll still be seeking vengeance there, as well.

Broken Bridges

My body is old and close to returning to dust.
For my survival, supplemental oxygen is a must.
My skin is loose and filled with ridges.
And my memory exhibits several broken bridges.

I sit in this nursing home counting my breath.
But your assaulting me was worse than death.
I'm no different from your father, when he gets old and frail.
I hope that you spend the rest of your life in jail.

Mental Blender

It's good to keep things in the family,
But some branches belong on a different tree.
Family members should be trusted,
Which is why what you did makes me feel disgusted.

It is disputed whether people are born gay.
When I was three, you made me that way.
For you, the opportunity was golden.
For me, my innocence was stolen.

Performing sexual acts at that age put my mind in a blender,
Especially because we are the same gender.
Some young people experiment to see what sex is like,
But you taught me these things before I even knew how to ride a
bike.

I refuse to keep silent any longer.
Revealing what you did to me made me stronger.

Broken

I know I come across as strong and outspoken,
But on the inside I'm really broken.
I often thought that no one really cared,
So my pain was never shared.
But when I revealed it for the world to see,
I realized that it had happened to others besides me.

One More Day

I carried a tremendous level of responsibility.

To spare my younger sister, I suggested instead that you molest me.

Even though my experiences were extremely rough,

I prayed that I would be more than enough.

Given everything that you put me through,

I couldn't bear the thought of her going through it, too.

With me, you can have your way,

If it will buy my little sister one more day.

Mole

For weeks as I walked,
I had no idea that I was being stalked.
I had been trapped.
I disappeared when I was kidnapped.

He wanted my goods,
So he took me deep into the woods.
Down below we would hunker
Into a hellish bunker.

He violated me several times each day—
And in every imaginable way.
It wasn't as bad as it might have seemed.
For freedom is what I dreamed.
I awoke in a very dark hole,
Where I was forced to live like a mole.

Do you see me as an animal? What the heck?!
You abuse me with this chain wrapped around my neck!
I felt like I was damned.
When I got his gun, I tried to fire, but it jammed.

Thank You, Lord. I wouldn't have survived without You.
When I got hold of his cell phone, You ensured my message got through.
After a week of my being repeatedly raped,
You opened the way and I finally escaped.

Still, I cried a great number of tears
When he was sentenced to a few hundred years.

Note: Inspired by Investigation Discovery's *Surviving Evil.*

Extra Credit

I used to say, "My parents didn't raise a fool!"
But this isn't high school.
Going to college is now something I regret
Because I learned a lesson I'll never forget.

I trusted God and my friend, too.
I hadn't thought this to be something that a friend would do.
Finally, someone older who could buy me a drink!
Little did I know that he'd use alcohol to push me over the brink.

Friends to the end is what we were supposed to be.
But look where trusting you got me.

International Incident

Foreign exchange meant something different to me.
It was a chance to learn in, and discover, another country.
I thought I was going to have the time of my life.
I never knew that I would be abused by a husband and wife.

No one told me that this was a price I had to pay.
I knew that I couldn't stay.
My ambassador blew a fuse,
When she heard the disheartening news.

It could've started World War III—
That which you did to me.

Sold

My family was destitute
So they sold me as a child prostitute.
On the very first day, I knew I wouldn't win,
As you took turns "breaking me in."

Then you told me the price I'd have to pay
If I wanted to earn my freedom one day.
This gave me incentive to save.
I wanted to stop being your sex slave.

It was a despicable trade,
Because of the price those children paid.
Luckily, a few people cared,
Along with the police, who finally dared.

We lived in your prison without hope to flee
Until the authorities rescued me.
But there's one thing that I don't know.
Since my parents sold me, where do I go?!

Occupational Hazard

For a fee, I show you a very good time.
But you committed a worse crime.
When you drove me to my special nook,
My money wasn't the only thing you took.

And to add to this night's curse,
My pimp's missing money made things worse.
When I told my pimp what I had gone through,
He said, "Where's my money? I don't care about you!"

Now I really need some medical care.
Also, is this a story the police want to hear?
I feel that my mind and body have been beaten with sticks.
But it's now back to work to turn some tricks.

Veal

In some countries, children push dolls in a baby carriage.
But here, we are sold into marriage.
For some, the future looks great.
But not for me. Today is my wedding. I'm only eight.
Here, it's a rare scene
To see a single girl under the age of fifteen.
And, yes, what you're thinking is right:
I have to fulfill my "wifely duties" tonight.
I've prayed and I've cried
Because so many young girls have died.
Today is the beginning of my life's painful reality.
I have a forty-year-old husband as the head of my family.
He rules the house with a whip and a rod,
And somehow he still worships God.

I can't believe that my parents were so cold.
I was their property, so I was sold.
I'm not sure I'm able, but I know I'm not willing.
Still, I must do my duty or the consequences will be chilling.
I hope that he tempers his zeal
And that, before the next time, he allows me to heal.

Special Award

The only thing worse than rape

Is when the perpetrators put it on tape.

I'm not talking about movies that simulate.

I'm talking about when people actually violate.

It's bad enough when rape endures in a survivor's memory,

But the indignity is worsened when the act is available for others
to see.

When they record it so that they can later offer a critique,

The death penalty must be the award that they seek.

Have people forgotten that rape is a crime?

I hope that they'll remember this fact when doing hard time.

Not in Vain

Six men caused her to lose her breath.
A court in India said that they deserved death.
Her case led many to blow a fuse,
As the rapists despicable acts had made international news.

With a friend, she caught a bus to take her home,
But she ended up dying alone.
Even though she lost her life,
She shed light on women's strife.

Some call her a hero.
It's sad that her case didn't reduce the incidence of rape to zero.
Her family's life is not the same.
But thank the Lord that she didn't die in vain.

Shame

What you did left me broken.
I couldn't heal as long as my shame remained unspoken.
My burdens lessened to very few
When I realized that the shame was on you.

The thing that really helped me during my plight
Was dousing my shame in light.

Anniversary

Anniversaries are usually filled with cheer,
Especially after the first year.
But, as my confidants can see,
This is not a happy time for me.

I wish that these things would fade to black,
But the fact is that my memories keep coming back.
My physical wounds healed just fine.
However, my invisible wounds need more time.

So, this anniversary doesn't come happily.
After all this time, I remember what you did to me.
Yet, despite my having been struck by this lightning rod,
I still believe and trust in God.

Surreal Ordeal

Where, exactly, do I start?
Maybe with the day he tore my family apart?
I was kidnapped from my bedroom.
He was married, but I became the temporary bride of this "groom."
It didn't matter to him that I was underage.
I was too young to go to that stage.
Nor did securing my consent matter.
I was his daily bread on a platter.

My body shivered in the freezing rain
As he secured me to a tree with a chain.
We basically hid in plain sight.
Secured by an invisible chain that he held tight.

Luckily, one day I met a stranger
Who simply knew that I was in danger.
But that wasn't the day the saga ended.
Ten years later, some of my wounds remain unmended.

It was an incredible ordeal
That makes my life seem surreal.
I was a child—young and frail.
But now he's the child, rotting in jail.

What Doesn't Kill You . . .

What doesn't kill you usually makes you strong.
But this is killing me; I know it's wrong.
You are nearly twice my age.
Your touching me like that fills me with rage.

I'm not even sure if God will allow you to repent
For abusing someone too young to consent.
One of the greatest sources of my shame
Was the thought that I was to blame.

But one of the things I most regret
Was carrying on like it was something I could simply forget.
I'm forever scarred in my soul,
But I won't let your crime take control.

Sleep Tight

I find it hard to sleep at night,
Not because I had to fight.
It's not so much that this happened to me;
Rather, it's because of my child's proximity.

My memories were swept away with my mind's broom,
But my child heard everything from the next room.
When I kiss him and say, "Sleep tight,"
I know that he's haunted by what he heard that night.

One of the reasons I didn't cower
Was to save him, and the thought gave me power.
What had happened to me
Was about to become his destiny.

It was better to "take one for the team"
Than for my son to share this bad dream.

Reclaimed Property

Your greatest felony
Was thinking that you owned me.
You took what I didn't want to give,
But you couldn't take away my will to live.

That day in court,
Giving me that look was your last resort.
The way you looked at me
Like I was your property.
But what you couldn't see
Was that you no longer had control over me.

It took some time before I went on a date.
But you had one that first night with your cellmate.
As what you did to me begins to fade away,
You still have hell to pay.

Every Breath

I was rescued, but nothing really mattered.
Life as I knew it had been totally shattered.
I was at the end of my rope.
My life was filled with pain. I had no hope.
While I cannot say that I thrived,
I can say that I am happy to have survived.

After being raped and threatened with death,
I now enjoy taking every single breath.

Never Broken

You treated me like a horse you were trying to break.
You thought that raping me was all it would take.
You ruthlessly exerted your power,
Making me go for days without taking a shower.

Then things got really strange
When you, a monster, suddenly decided to change.
When you asked if I wanted to give sex a go,
Being raped was my other option, so I didn't say no.

Even though you entered me "consensually,"
It was no different from what you had previously done to me.
It was really sick and sad
That you thought I was going to say that you were the best I'd
ever had.

And when you held me "romantically" while you slept,
I shed no tears, though all night I wept.
Once I saw my chance to get free,
I knew it would be the last time you would ever see me.

You took a part of me, physically,
But my love can only be given by me.
You insinuated that we were going to be husband and wife.
Sweet dreams to you as you remain in prison for the rest of your life.

Note: Inspired by Investigation Discovery's *Surviving Evil.*

Mud

The officer thought that my face was covered in mud
Until the light showed that it was really dried blood.
But no words were spoken,
As the bones in my face had been brutally broken.

Inside and outside, I bled
After being beaten, raped, and left for dead.
Like the apostle Paul, I was beaten nearly to death,
But the Lord restored my breath.

Because of the damage to my body he had produced,
A coma was medically induced.
Then I miraculously opened my eyes.
News of his capture came as a pleasant surprise.
But there was no time for me to weep.
I was exhausted and needed to sleep.

I remember something the detective had said
About seeing less traumatic wounds on those who had ended up
dead.
That night wasn't my time.
Now I'm free. He will spend his life paying for his crime.

Note: Inspired by Investigation Discovery's *Surviving Evil*.

False Claim

When parents are asleep or away,
Their kids may get into mischief during their play.
For some minors, this means "scoring" quicker
By supplying heavy doses of liquor.

The need for a legal age to drink
Makes more sense than you might think.
Some can't wait for that day,
So others use alcohol to entice their prey.

And after getting a child into a predicament,
They'll claim that they were given consent.
But when someone is too drunk to say no,
It's a stoplight: don't go.

Alcohol, often a component of having a "good time",
Is frequently used in the commission of a despicable crime.

More than You Bargained For

I begged you, "No, stop, please!"
You had no idea that I had a disease.
You went after what you could see,
But it wasn't apparent to you that I had HIV.

You chose to continue despite my pleas.
Welcome to a life with herpes.
You put me through hell and have no regrets.
I gave you some parting gifts that you'll never forget.

I remember your rage when I told you no.
Now I get to say that I told you so.

Salt

My wounds have been washed of the salt.
Now I know that it wasn't my fault.

About the Author

Kollin L. Taylor went through a heartbreaking experience that brought him closer to God (his ultimate source of strength and inspiration) and launched his writing career. Kollin has written enough material for thirty-eight books, twenty-four of which have been published. Within the space of fourteen months, he was inspired to write more than thirteen hundred poems, which is why Chaplain Robert A. Miller calls him the Phenom. While he hopes that others do not begin writing for the reasons he did, he bravely shares some of his life's journey in the following books:

Exposed Part I: The Prelude
Exposed Part II: Romantic Relationships
Exposed Part III: Vida
Exposed Part IV: The Journey Continues
Metamorphosis: The New Me
The Phenom: From My Soul
Resilience: Bend, Don't Break
The Aftermath: When the Smoke Clears and the Dust Settles
Perspective: A New Point of View
The Anatomy of a Heartbreak: When Samson Met Delilah (narrative)
Round 2: The Battle Continues
Round 3: Still Fighting
Cool Breeze: Irie Man
Finding Joy in You: The Gift of Eternal Life
Minister to the People: Answering His Calling
The Path to Enlightenment

Knowledge Is Power: Before You Do What You're Told, Know What You're Being Told

Soul Food: Thanks, Lord, for My Daily Bread

Closet Christian: If You Deny Him, He Will Deny You

Australia: A Journey Down Under

Wrongfully Accused: When Innocence Is Not Enough

The Sidelines: Those Who Can . . .

Flirting with Disaster

The Sound of a Fallen Tree

Survival is his twenty-fifth book and his twenty-fourth poetry book.

Author photo by Sterlin King.

Connect with the author on Facebook at
https://www.facebook.com/KollinLTaylor.